IMAGES
of America

MERIDIAN
STREET

At both the north and south boundaries of the Meridian Street Historic District, motorists and pedestrians alike are greeted by these markers. The gold lettering and deep blue enamel backgrounds symbolize the state flag of Indiana. The signs warmly welcome all who pass to "One of America's Great Streets." (Author's collection.)

ON THE COVER: The old Governor's Mansion is pictured as it appeared in 1945 when Gov. Ralph Gates and his wife, Helene, moved in as the first first family of Indiana to take up residence at 4343 North Meridian Street. (Courtesy of Marjie Gates Giffin.)

IMAGES
of America

MERIDIAN
STREET

Kassie Ritman

ARCADIA
PUBLISHING

Published by Arcadia Publishing
Charleston, South Carolina

Printed in the United States of America

Library of Congress Control Number: 2019940206

For all general information, please contact Arcadia Publishing:
Telephone 843-853-2070
Fax 843-853-0044
E-mail sales@arcadiapublishing.com
For customer service and orders:
Toll-Free 1-888-313-2665

Visit us on the Internet at www.arcadiapublishing.com

Dedicated to my family, who endured stacks of "Meridian stuff" everywhere, and to my personal cheerleaders Enid Cokinos, Marjie Gates Giffin, and Judy Miller, who never quit pushing.

CONTENTS

ACKNOWLEDGMENTS

A complete and separate volume would be called for to personally thank all of those who aided me in gathering these photographs and small stories. Bringing the houses of Meridian Street to life as the family homes they are has been a four-year odyssey. I am truly grateful to three outstanding women, Elaine Klein, JoAnn "Jodi" McLane, and Peggy Sabens. Between them, they have lived on the street for nearly 150 years. With enthusiasm, they opened their doors to me, answered endless questions, and guided me toward written materials, scrapbooks, and doorsteps of others who could help. While living busy lives and raising their families, they stood witness to the near fall of this grand section of our city to commercial encroachment. In response, they rallied the help of neighbors and city officials in an initiative to stop "progress" from overrunning the historical and aesthetic importance of this neighborhood. They are a blessing to their spouses, families, and Indianapolis as a whole.

Unless otherwise noted, all images in this work are from the private collection of the author.

INTRODUCTION

Around 1900, Meridian Street north of Maple Road (now Thirty-Eighth Street) was a single-width dirt lane outside of the original city limits. Meanwhile, Indianapolis proper was bustling with traction cars, steam trains, canal barges, and healthy industrial concerns. All of this modernization in the city known as "the Crossroads of America" created a great deal of pollution and noise. Those who built their fortunes and homes within the city limits were rethinking the elaborate Victorian mansions that were falling out of style, and looking to the countryside for an escape.

Although many wealthy families summered in the lakes region of northern Indiana (Wawasee being a favorite) or farther up in Michigan, a getaway that was also a year-round home became fashionable. Owners of farmland and orchards north of Maple Road soon began selling off lots to those eager to escape the oppressive heat and foul smells emanating from nonrefrigerated slaughterhouses and industrial plants.

Initially, a handful of weekend residences were built (the current garage at 4343 being one of the remaining structures). Then came informal, yet quite sizable, country homes inspired by farmhouses. About 25 homes were put up before 1920. Most of these early houses were not designed by local architects but were selected from upscale catalogues of home plan designs. Meridian Street addresses as "must have" badges of achievement for families of means really took off in the 1920s. The popularity of the Meridian dream spurred many to begin buying up lots and start a business of building massive houses on speculation. In fact, during the 1920s and 1930s, a whopping 118 of the 176 structures (about two-thirds) within the historic district were constructed.

Building on Meridian Street hit an economic wall in the 1940s as the country was consumed with another world war. Only eight homes were built in this decade. But a surge—albeit an initially unwelcome one—happened in the 1950s. Twenty-four new homes began inserting themselves on the empty lots between the whimsical and classically styled mansions Meridian Street was so highly regarded for. Most of these homes were of the one-story ranch style reflective of the nation's postwar craving for mid-century modern homes with new conveniences and streamlined living.

After this postwar boom, the neighborhood was in danger of destruction. The Hare-Tarkington home, at 4270, was sold to a group hoping to convert the genteel cottage into a nightclub. The historically significant house at 4020 was built by the Frank Flanner family and was subsequently home to Indianapolis Motor Speedway cofounder Arthur Newby as well as Roy Brandt, manufacturer of the Indianapolis Car Company. It was demolished to make way for the Tarkington Tower apartment project. At the same time, several homes along the street were in use as rentals, and more than a handful were being used as offices rather than homes. The outlook was dismal.

In 1960, the Meridian Street Foundation was formed to combat such encroachments. Though it fought the Tarkington Tower apartment project in court for several years, eventually developer Jack Weldon won out, and the project proceeded (Tarkington is now condominiums).

During the next several years, many more properties were endangered, and the foundation was able to preserve most of them with the help of street resident Jack Schaller, who bought up empty homes and spared them from demise.

By the 1980s, it was apparent that stronger measures were necessary if the integrity of Meridian Street was to be preserved. A stout group of residents began the arduous task of having the entire stretch from Fortieth Street to the Indianapolis Central Canal listed in the National Register of Historic Places. This included all 175 contributing and noncontributing structures as well as the street itself. On the original nomination form, submitted in 1986 to the National Park Service on behalf of North Meridian Historic District, the 10th item, "Verbal Description and Boundaries," lays out the extent of the district:

> The North Meridian Street Historic District consists of properties located along the east and west sides of North Meridian Street. The boundary specifically begins at the northern curb of 40th Street and follows the rear property lines of the houses located on the east and west sides of the street. The boundary continues in a northerly direction across 42nd Street on the west; 43rd Street on the east; Hampton Drive on the west; 45th Street and Meridian Place on the east, 46th, 49th, 52nd, and 56th Streets on the east and west; and 57th Street on the east. The northern end of the boundary is formed by the southern curb of Westfield Boulevard on the west, and the southern curb of Meridian Lane on the east.

Once approval was granted, the threat of further commercial, multi-family, or nonresidential usage was abated. There is even an agreement in place that if at any time the beloved restaurant at the district's north tip (the Meridian) ever ceases operation, it will revert to approved use as a residence only.

Additionally, some individual structures on Meridian Street have sought and been granted separate listing status in the National Register by the National Park Service. The former Governor's Mansion at 4343 is listed, and the current owners are also in the application process to have the master bath entered as a separate component (the tile work, stained-glass ceiling, and general amenities are amazing and certainly worthy of protection). The Cole house at 4909, built by the owner of the Cole Automobile Company, achieved its own protected status under the foresight of previous owners Frank and Patte Owings. Even the massive limestone wall with bronzed fencing and double gate at 5323 have been gifted to Historic Landmarks Indiana as an easement to preserve the pure art of this streetside embellishment.

One of Meridian Street's most beloved sons, author Booth Tarkington, writing for the *Saturday Evening Post*, said of his neighborhood in "The World Does Move":

> The houses upon this new street—all built within little more than a year—were of the newest fashions, yet not many were of the same fashion. They were of shape and colors we once should have thought fanciful; indeed, many of them suggested stage settings, and their picturesqueness was so extreme as to give them almost the unsubstantial air of picture book houses. It was obvious that every architect or every owner had planned without thought to what would neighbor the new houses.

What a lovely way to describe an amazing collection of homes and history.

One

FROM FORTIETH STREET TO FORTY-THIRD STREET

When touring Meridian Street from the south, the home formerly addressed as 4020 will not be seen. The substantial country home was built in 1899 by Frank Flanner (of Flanner Buchanan) for his family. Although home to many familiar Indianapolis names while it existed, the house and extensive gardens around it were demolished in 1965 to make way for Tarkington Towers. In this c. 1940s photograph, the south facade of the home shows the original fieldstone banding. (Courtesy of the Campaigne family.)

Automobile racing enthusiast and cofounder of the Indianapolis Motor Speedway Arthur Newby purchased the home in 1906. He funded the luxurious address by manufacturing popular automobiles as owner of National Motor Car & Vehicle Corporation and the Diamond Chain Company. Pictured here is the interior of his spacious home and the decor typical of the time. (Courtesy of the Campaigne family.)

The heavily contested multifamily residence Tarkington Towers is a luxury condominium filled with amenities for nearly 100 units in 16 stories. Despite efforts by the Meridian Street Foundation (established in 1960 to preserve the historic and aesthetic integrity of Meridian Street from Fortieth Street north to the canal), the tower was built in 1968. The tower was designed by Robert Longardner & Associates and built by developer Jack Weldon. By design, the Tarkington maintained a portion of the fieldstone wall erected by Flanner as a decorative marker for his property line. The wall remains intact at the north end bordering Fortieth Street and for a bit along the Meridian Street approach as well.

In 1908, the first of many English cottage–style homes was erected at 4001 North Meridian Street. Although "cottage" might conjure visions of small charming abodes, these were substantially sized homes with a generous helping of decorative flourish. Half-timbering, fancy brickwork, and a variety of windows and rooflines made these large homes feel quaint and inviting. Attorney John Hollett and his wife, Katherine, daughter of two-term Indianapolis mayor Tom Sullivan, kept the home in their family for more than 40 years.

Built in 1921 for realtor Maurice Tibbs, who only owned the home for about a year, 4011 saw three more changes of ownership over the next 30 years. In 1951, the James L. Beattey family moved in and stayed for 10 full years. Beattey was an attorney and director of the Standard Life Insurance Company. He served as secretary to the Democratic State Committee and was manager of the Indiana State Fair. After the Beattey family moved in 1961, the house was used as a rental until recent years despite its charming French chateau styling and flourish.

With a nod to the Italian High Renaissance style, 4025 was designed by prolific local architect Merritt Harrison in 1923. Harrison was also responsible for the Indiana State Fairgrounds Coliseum design. Dr. William F. Hughes and his wife, Alta, were the first owners.

Before the advent of in-home refrigerators, homes depended on deliveries from local ice vendors to keep perishables cool in wooden ice boxes. As this unidentified baby at 4136 has a relaxing bath in the sink, the ice delivery door at right stands ready to be filled without disturbing residents with a pre-dawn knock on the door. (Courtesy of Paul B. Schaller.)

Another of Harrison's designs, 4041 showcases his knowledge of classic design. This stunner is rendered as a Jacobean, with tall banks of windows and an impossibly steep slate-covered roof stealing the aesthetic show. William R. and Sarah Adams were the first occupants. His mother and a housemaid lived with them. He worked as a streetcar conductor.

The striking symmetry of 4045 gives this Frank B. Hunter–designed Colonial a timeless appeal. Norman Metzger (secretary-treasurer of the Indiana Terminal Warehouse) and his wife, Mary, commissioned the home in 1916. After the 1940s, it fell into the trap of becoming a rental property, a fate it suffered for the next 50 years. Finally, around 1990, the home was purchased and restored.

Frederick Jungclaus, son of prolific developer and contractor William Jungclaus, owned 4057. He began his career in construction working for his father as a carpenter's apprentice. Over the years, he learned construction literally from the ground up. He headed the successful firm, following in the footsteps of his father. Jungclaus was injured in a car accident at the age of 87. His wife was already hospitalized at the time of his crash and tragically passed the very next day. Frederick was hospitalized for about a month before succumbing to complications of his injuries.

William Jungclaus, father of Frederick, founded the Indianapolis construction firm that built many landmark buildings. Among those attributed to Jungclaus are the H.P. Wasson department store, the English Hotel, the Stutz Motor Car Company, and the Real Silk Hosiery Mill. Perhaps the most recognizable of these were the Circle Tower and the Murat Shrine. Jungclaus made his home at 4061, next door to his son and grandchildren. The firm continues today as Jungclaus Campbell.

Built as one of two duplexes in the historic district, 4118 was originally a multifamily dwelling. In lieu of the popular side-by-side styling for most "doubles," architects George & MacLucas designed the living quarters for client Sol Meyer as separate first-floor and second-floor dwellings. Harry Herff, who founded the Herff-Jones Company with partner Randall Jones, lived at this address for many years. Their firm makes championship rings for the Indy 500 and Super Bowl, along with trophies such as the college basketball Naismith Award.

Next door is the other duplex, also in an "up and down" configuration. Sol Meyer commissioned the same architect to design 4122. His purpose for building the duplexes was to easily house his and his wife's families. The resemblance to banks built in this era (around 1922) is not surprising, as Sol Meyer was a prominent Indianapolis banker.

Reserve Loan Life Insurance Company president William Zulich lived at 4127 from 1919 until 1933. The Colonial exterior made a sturdy and conservative statement for Zulich, whose business was built on his own reputation as well as the perceived financial soundness of his company.

The charming two-story home at 4130 was built in 1911, when simpler, more farmhouse-influenced styles prevailed. The Eugene Stuart family owned the home into the mid-1940s. Stuart was a druggist who owned a small local chain of neighborhood drugstores.

Pictured here around 1918, the Moos (later Moss) sisters line up for a photograph. Their summer whites were typical clothing worn by women at home during the oppressive heat and humidity of Indianapolis summers. (Courtesy of the Dobson family.)

The home at 4131 served for a while as the administrative offices of the Norways Foundation. The private Indianapolis mental hospital was established for the treatment of brain injury and psychiatric patients in 1898. Dr. Phillip Reed, who lived in the home, was the medical director of Norways for more than 20 years. His wife, Genevieve, served as executive director. In 1957, after losing much of its patients to the newly opened and less expensive LaRue Carter Hospital, Norways closed. The Reeds left town and moved to Lafayette to work at Wabash Valley Sanitarium.

One of only two Frank Lloyd Wright–inspired Prairie homes on Meridian Street, 4136 was built with family living in mind. Beautifully symmetric and astonishingly modern in appearance, the home was designed by Fermor Spencer Cannon in 1923. (Courtesy of the Schaller family.)

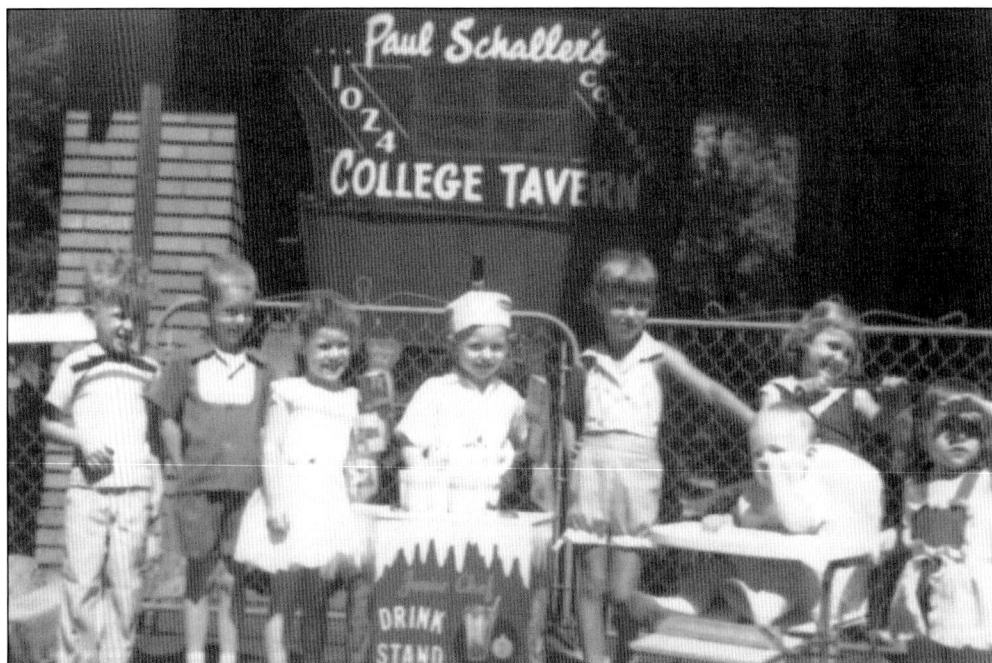

Local tavern owner Paul Schaller owned 4136 for nearly 40 years, from 1945 into the 1980s. His business, College Tavern, was a popular nightspot filled with live music and high-spirited patrons. The party didn't stop at the tavern for the Schaller family. Paul and Adalia were big fans of the Indianapolis 500 and hosted annual parties. Daughter Paula recalls guests like Roger Ward, Gene Genaro, and Tony Hulman stopping by for fun. Here, the Schaller kids and neighbors sell Kool Aid at a stand made for them by Paul. The family's red 1912 Parry Overland Model 61 touring car can be seen in the background. (Courtesy of the Schaller family.)

When Louis and Ava Borinstein built their home at 4137 in 1915, his brother and business partner Abe soon followed suit. The immigrant brothers amassed their fortune as junk dealers with large scrapyards for metal refuse. When the United States entered World War I, their junk became gold. Both brothers were well respected, as their wealth was equaled by their philanthropy. In 1929, they donated a building at 3516 Central for use as the Borinstein Home for the Aged (a forerunner of Hooverwood).

The home at 4142, finished in 1917, sat empty until it was purchased the following year by Isadore E. Solomon. Solomon was a clothing merchant who owned and managed the Rite's Shops. He and his wife, Pauline, raised their family here and remained in the home for 18 years.

A young Earl Newberry sits atop a "picture pony." These ponies brought up to North Meridian Street from poor parts of the city were a common sight during the Great Depression and through the World War II years. Families sent children to the wealthy area to offer "rich kids" a ride or a photograph in exchange for a few cents. (Courtesy of the Newberry family.)

Emil Rahke, president of the Silent Salesman Company, moved his family into 4146 in 1929. With business interests in food production and vending machines, he was able to ride out the Great Depression and kept the fashionable address for 20 years.

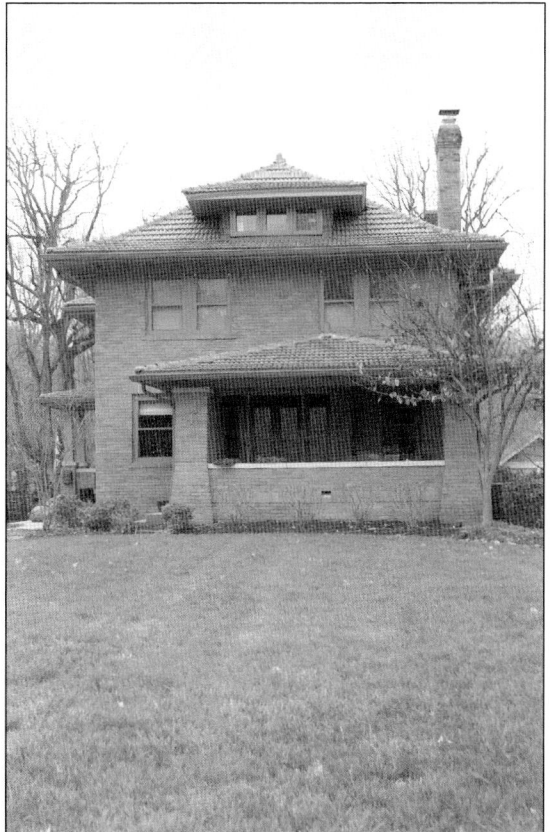

From its construction in 1917 for the Charles F. Voyles family, 4150 remained in the same family for nearly 100 years. Only the surname changed when it passed to the Blassingham family via Dr. Voyles's daughter's line. Voyles, who was a well-respected physician in Indianapolis, also held a coveted membership in the National Society of the Sons of the American Revolution.

Abe and Marguerite Borinstein began construction on their home at 4155 a few months after brother Louis started 4137. Orienting the home's front to face south rather than west toward Meridian street allowed the Borinsteins a bucolic view of the park-like lawn with ornamental plantings on the full city lot between the brothers' homes. The families maintained the mutual lawn space as a place for relaxation, entertainment, and a playground for their children.

Interior decorator Charles A. Edwards and his wife, Essie, purchased the home at 4156, built in 1924, and added flourish via furnishings over the next 16 years. Later, this was one of the Meridian homes nearly lost to commercial space. The Schoolcraft Company used it as offices in the mid-1960s. Fortunately, the home was bought in 1967 by Millard E. Wright, who lived in and revived the residential finishes to the home, sparing it from any further business use.

Frank and Mary Sudbrock moved one lot south of their previous home into 4162 in 1923 with Mary's widowed sister, Emilie, and her children in tow. Since Frank worked as a traveling salesman in the dry goods business, the living arrangements worked well. A close look at 4162 reveals a sort of trademark design element from architect D.A. Bohlen & Son. Limestone lintels over the lower windows and door serve as both structural and decorative elements. The unique use of structural limestone over the window of a residential building was repeated by Bohlen on most of the homes the firm designed.

In 1919, D.A. Bohlen & Son designed 4204 as a home to be enjoyed by families. The second owner, Carrie R. Rink, purchased the home from Frank H. Sudbrock in 1924 shortly after she was widowed. Known as a very independent woman in her day, Rink stayed in the large home without live-in help.

Built in 1924, the charming house at 4226 was first lived in by Augustus Early and his family. After only two years, Augustus contracted pneumonia and died. Brokenhearted, his wife, Della Belle, moved into the Marott Hotel at Meridian Street and Fall Creek Parkway and put the house up for sale. Timing was against her, as it took nearly five years to sell. Eventually she remarried. After two decades and three or four owners, Della Belle, again widowed, purchased 4226 again and was able to enjoy her beloved home for the last years of her life.

One of the oldest homes in the district is now barely visible from the street. The two-and-a-half-story, portico-fronted house was built in 1909 for the Dr. Joseph Stillson family. Dr. Stillson was one of the first physicians to specialize in ailments of the ear, nose, and throat. Sited on the largest lot on the street (an astounding five acres when it was built), 4245 is the epitome of "country in the city." Heavily wooded, the lawn is well suited to both privacy and refuge. Daughter Blanche Stillson was a naturalist who created a bird sanctuary via careful selection of plantings to create alluring habitats.

Another of the earliest builds on North Meridian Street, the cottage home of Maria Hare at 4270 is rumored to have been designed by the widow for the enjoyment of her six children. Heiress to a substantial grocery fortune, Hare was tragically widowed when her husband, Clinton, died shortly after the couple purchased the country land. In 1923, she was approached by prolific author Booth Tarkington, who was looking to move from his own longtime family home after the deaths of both his beloved father and only daughter within months of each other. The Tarkingtons held the property for nearly 30 years.

Engraved plaques stand beneath a pair of cherubs flanking the drive at 4270. The markers are a subtle confirmation to the curious that this house was indeed once Booth Tarkington's home.

Dr. LaRue D. Carter and his wife lived at 4280 from 1933 to 1945. Dr. Carter was a famous neuropsychiatrist. Despite a demanding private practice and numerous speaking engagements around the country, Dr. Carter also found time to teach at Indiana University Medical School. When a modern psychiatric hospital was opened in 1952, it was named LaRue D. Carter Memorial in honor of his numerous contributions to the care and treatment of those suffering mental and emotional illnesses.

Often referred to on home tours as "the Murder House," the Dell-Moffett house, at 4285, is a gloriously substantial American foursquare on a wide sweep of lot. Dell made his fortune in wholesale coal, while Paul G. Moffett served in the state legislature and listed his occupation as "farmer." Beginning in the 1950s, developer and land speculator Stanley Selig used the home as a base for his businesses. On March 10, 1970, a disgruntled investor who had traveled from Alaska burst into Selig's office and shot him five times at close range. Selig made it to the hospital but tragically died within minutes of arrival.

Passing in a car, one could easily miss 4290. The pretty home on a corner lot is oriented facing north toward Forty-Third Street. George and Margaret Kuhn ran a property management and real estate company. Likely the builders of the home, they lived in it for a year before renting it out. Finally, in 1920, the Kuhns moved in, staying for about a dozen years before selling it.

Two

4300 BLOCK NORTH TO FORTY-SIXTH STREET

The house at 4305 was quite controversial when proposed. Built in the 1950s, it was at the leading edge of the resurgence of Meridian Street addresses as status symbols. However, with its clearly different look, the contemporary home was sharply opposed by many. Finally, protesting neighbors relented as assurances were made that the home would be professionally designed and constructed from the highest-quality materials available. Or perhaps residents just grew weary of the fight and saw an influx of the wildly popular mid-century modern homes as inevitable on the remaining lots. In the end, 4305, with its artful design and detailed landscaping, was a big hit and a glad addition.

Designed by Rubush and Hunter, the George A. Gay house, at 4310, is an architectural cousin to Indianapolis landmarks the Columbia Club and the Circle Theater. Purchased in 1935, it became home to Phillip R. Mallory, chairman of P.R. Mallory Company. Mallory ran his empire of battery, timer, and machine part manufacturing plants from a downtown Indianapolis headquarters.

Built in 1917, the Frank P. Fox house, at 4311, mixed cottage charm with Craftsman styling. It is believed that Fox himself acted as the home's designer and builder. An early celebrity in motor sports, he piloted his personal automobile, a Pope-Hartford, in the inaugural Indianapolis 500 in 1911. Fox started in row two and finished 22nd after completing 162 laps by the time the checkered flag dropped. In spite of having an artificial leg, he was considered one of the fiercest and hardest-driving racers of the day and was especially respected for his talents. Frank Fox was also the Indianapolis dealer of the Pope-Hartford Automobile Company (manufactured from 1905 until 1913).

Built of brick, timber, stucco, and limestone, the house at 4320 was first owned by wholesale coal dealer Roy C. Bain in 1929. Later, it was home base for the William D. Ruckelshaus family from 1967 to 1971. Ruckelshaus, an attorney, came into national prominence when tapped by President Nixon to head the newly created Environmental Protection Agency. Later, he filled an interim role as director of the FBI and served as deputy attorney general of the United States.

The long, low silhouette of 4330 was a shocking addition to neighbors when it broke the 20-year hiatus of new construction on the block. Just like the other ranch homes that began populating vacant lots, the Bert I. Sexson home was not warmly welcomed by the old guard. But times were changing, and women's magazines were heavily influencing this type of home as current, efficient, and desirable.

After World War II, the house rented by the state at 101 West Twenty-Seventh Street as the official home and residence of the sitting governor had fallen into sorry shape. The legislature approved $72,500 for the purchase of 4343 (seen here and on the cover). This impressive house was custom built in 1924 for Stutz Motor Car Company president William Thompson. In 1945, the newly inaugurated governor, Ralph Gates, and his wife, Helene, took up residence with their family. The elegant buff brick and green-tiled roof made a grand statement to Indiana's residents and visitors alike. Even the wrought iron fence pickets were gold-leafed at their tips. The setting and landscaping were tastefully formal without seeming arrogant. It was an impressive home for Indiana's highest-ranking politician. However, to the dismay of those early residents, the home may have seemed a bit too inviting. People often came to the door uninvited or simply walked in as if entering a downtown office building instead of a private family home. Many went so far as to pocket personal belongings of the governor's family while inside the house as souvenirs, while others boldly picked flowers out of the yard.

Here, Gov. Ralph and Helene Gates pose before a formal dinner party begins. The new mansion was well suited to entertaining, as the dining room accommodates a table for 24. The entry hall was also quite grand and is rumored to have once hosted Roy Rogers and Dale Evans, who, to the delight of invited dignitaries, stood in the entryway with their horses and signed autographs for adults and children alike. (Courtesy of Marjie Gates Giffin.)

Eager costumed revelers stop for a group photograph just before setting out on their annual treat-gathering mission. Per legend, each governor was judged by the children of the neighborhood as either a good or bad leader according to the Halloween treats handed out. One governor (the teller of this story did not reveal the name or political affiliation) was instantly deemed unworthy for office when sandwich bags containing one graham cracker per kid were the healthy alternative doled out to trick-or-treaters. (Courtesy of Paula Schaller Roberts.)

Architect Bennett Kay designed 4350 at the height of the Meridian Street building frenzy. Of the original 175 structures inventoried on the application for listing in the National Register of Historic Places, 84 of them (about 40 percent) were built in the 1920s. From 1947 until 1957, Maurice and Rose Atlas lived in this home. Maurice owned a chain of six Atlas grocery stores, including the beloved location at Fifty-Fourth Street and College Avenue. The small neighborhood store gained national attention as David Letterman often mentioned his days as a bag boy there. Maurice and Rose were blessed to celebrate their 77th wedding anniversary before his passing in 1999.

The eye-catching home at 4356 was owned by the Zazas family across four decades. No detail was overlooked nor expense spared to beautify the Renaissance Revival manse. John Zazas contracted artisans directly from Europe to do special plaster work, decorative painting, stone carving, and sculpting. Zazas was known widely for his generosity and was honored by King Paul I of Greece for his donation of a school in his native village of Kandila. Several residents also speak of his funding to bring electrical service to the same village many years prior. Ironically, he never returned to Kandila as an adult.

Nicknamed "the Airplane House" for its perfectly aligned banks of windows and long, low profile like outstretched wings, 4366 is one of two Prairie-style homes in the district. The very modern-appearing home was designed in 1921 by the talented Frank B. Hunter for investment banker Wesley Shea. True to the vision of Frank Lloyd Wright, the home blends seamlessly into the lot's landscaping.

The Walk house was among the earliest homes on the stretch of Meridian Street north of Maple Road (now Thirty-Eighth Street). Built in 1911, the home at 4375 is nicely sited on a lightly sloping lot. Adolf Scherrer designed the home for Carl F. Walk, owner of the Walk Jewelry store. Walk built the business, founded by his father, Julius, to include luxury items such as home silver in addition to diamonds and fine watches. In 1941, Walk sold his store to the William H. Block department store, which continued it as a curated collection known as C. Walk inside the Block store.

Orlando B. and Ester Iles directed Meyers and Coffin to give them a large English cottage at 4400 that would appear small from the street. It was built in 1922, and a renovation took place shortly after completion. The roofline was raised and reworked, and an imposing tower with a copper-clad conical top was added. These changes switched the appearance from demure to bold and from cozy English to a home more likely to be found in the French countryside. Since 1964, the original "show home" on Meridian has been under the loving care of the William J. McLane family.

The home at 4401 is wide and tall, with a rather flat facade broken up by well-sized and -placed windows and asymmetrical wings flanking the north and south ends. A project of Frank B. Hunter, the home was built in 1923 but sat unsold until 1926. Banker Edwin H. Forry and his wife, Carrie (daughter of another prominent banker, Volney T. Mallott), moved into the home in 1929. Carrie Forry maintained her residence there until 1952.

Frank B. Hunter designed 4403 for the president and founder of Progress Laundry Company, Roy C. Shaneberger, in 1923. The commercial laundry service operated five plants in Indianapolis. An earnings statement from 1943, a very dismal year for most, showed the company made gross sales of $1.7 million with a net profit of just under $100,000. The 2019 equivalent would be sales of about $25 million with a profit of just under $1.5 million.

Dudley R. Gallahue enjoyed life at 4404 for 36 years. Widely known for his philanthropy, the founder and chairman of American States Insurance was diligent in his charitable works. A supporter of the Boys Club, Children's Museum, Boy Scouts, and Pals Club, Gallahue was even awarded status as an honorary Girl Scout. During his time on Meridian Street, the energetic retiree put an extensive formal garden in his backyard. It was made of a series of winding paths, each one leading to a specially themed "room" with bird feeders at every turn.

Lucius French wore many hats, from car dealer to architect. He designed and built this Tudor interpretation for himself at 4409 in 1924. Later, the director of Indiana National Bank and president of the traction company Interstate Car, Eugene Darrach, bought the elegant home.

Having moved to Indianapolis from the small southern Indiana town of Napoleon, Darrach's wife must have found the shopping and lifestyle quite exciting. Maude is seen here in one of her elaborate dresses. Certainly the department and specialty stores available to her upon moving north had to have been a welcome distraction. (Courtesy of Heather Broell.)

The end-to-end porch and two-story portico earned 4411 the nickname "the Southern Colonial." To Dr. Wells M. Osborn and his family, it was home. Later, evangelist Howard Cadle moved to the home. Known far and wide for his syndicated Sunday evening sermons, Cadle was a mainstay in homes across the nation as families gathered around their radio sets. Even a former boxer-turned-gangster credited a Cadle sermon broadcast for his surrender and confession in a $21,000 theft from the Beverly Hills Country Club.

Two years after 4414 was built, Earl W. Kiger bought the home in 1927. The owner of a large school supply house, Kiger sold everything any school from kindergarten to college could ever need, from crayons to American flags and school desks. Osler & Burns served as the architects.

The sweeping roofline of 4420 curves lightly as it comes over the airy screened porch. In Craftsman style, the home shows a half-timbering treatment, multiple window configurations and styles, and dormers and beams all competing for attention. The result is an incredibly charming home that looks to have evolved over many years. It was, in fact, all built in 1927. Jackson K. Ehlert, the first dean of the Jordan School of Music at Butler University, lived in the home with his wife, Marjorie, from 1958 to 1982.

Albert Goldstein, founder of the Goldstein Brothers Home Furnishings Company, commissioned Frank B. Hunter in 1926 to build a cozy Tudor for his family at 4425. Giving off the appearance of having a moat, with its entry level supported over a stone under-porch and dual stairways flanking a stone grotto, the Goldstein home is one of the most unique and adored on the street.

Everett Crabb designed and built 4430 in 1926 for Harry H. Pointer. Pointer only lived in the house for a few months before falling in love with an English cottage around the corner and moving. Dr. Charles and Sarah Newby Test purchased the home and lived in it from 1952 through the next several decades.

The McKee house, built in 1926 at 4450, is one of several homes with its front door perpendicular to the increasingly traffic-laden Meridian Street. By the late 1920s, most families living north of Thirty-Eighth Street owned one or more cars. Additionally, there was a lot of commercial traffic supporting these large homes. The iceman was a daily fixture moving along the street at dawn, filling orders indicated by large cards placed in the front window each morning by house staff. These were coded for the iceman to know what size ice block was desired to keep household perishables cool before in-home refrigerators were common. Coal, gasoline, milk, and laundry deliveries were part of everyday life. Meridian Street was busy and often loud.

The house at 4455 is unusual in the district, as it is a miniature version of the grander neighbors around it. Louise Duck, widow of Berkley, built it in 1942 to downsize from the much larger 5111 while still staying close to friends and neighbors. It is in the style of most two-story homes just north of the district around this time.

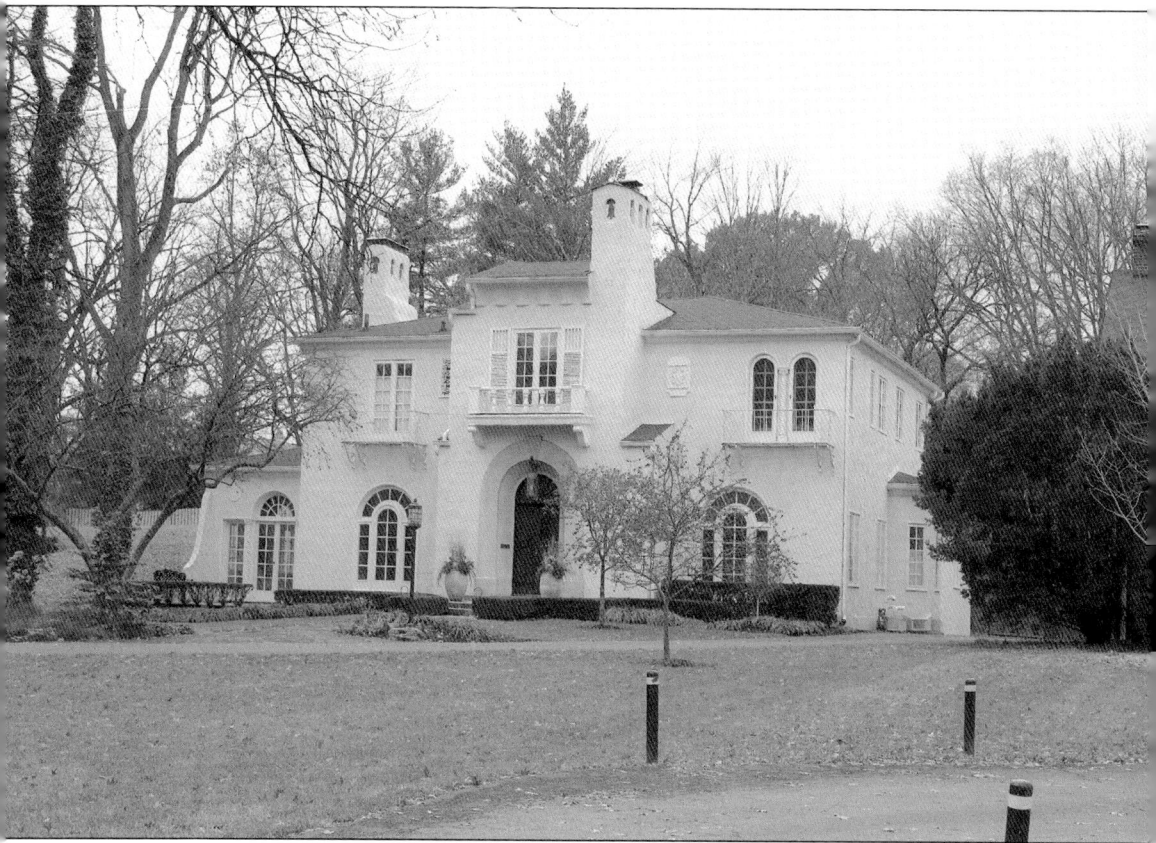

Commissioned by Dr. J.H. Kemper in 1928, the home at 4456 exudes a unique Spanish vibe with elements mixing formality and villa-like coziness. The original stucco finish was not white; rather, it was applied in four colors to accent features. The home was a mix of yellow, green, blue, and red-toned stucco topped with a red-tile roof. A massive iron chandelier fitted with red bulbs designed to replicate flickering candles greeted visitors inside the entry.

Another of the scaled-down versions of the more elaborate homes built previously, 4465 came along in 1941. Although smaller and less grand than most of the houses surrounding it, the Harold H. Wells house holds its own on the charm and elegance scale. The home is simple but built with a keen eye to proportion, and the decorative elements are clean and serve a purpose as well as aesthetic appeal.

The house at 4475 faces the small connector Forty-Fifth Street. Added to Meridian Street in 1940, it has the All-American look so popular at the time. This pleasing design lacks the showy grandeur of the mansions built during the boom years of the 1920s and 1930s but nevertheless is well landscaped and appealing in its appearance.

Another of the grand Colonials so popular in the late 1920s is the Mooney-Mericle House at 4480. William H. and Mary Mooney were the second owners. He was president of Cincinnati Development, a firm specializing in electrical and fiberglass products. Later, physician Earl W. Mericle owned the house for several years.

Though it was home to beloved children's dentist Dr. Betty Koss and her mother, Alice E. Koss, for many years, Frank B. Hunter originally designed 4501 in 1916 for another woman, Josephine Frommeyer. The subtle detailing of the facade keeps this home looking rather contemporary, even now that its 100th birthday has passed. It is a standout for its current blue color—the shade is subtle and allows this very large home to recede into the heavily landscaped lawn with quiet grace.

One of the larger homes on Meridian Street is at 4510. Built in 1931, the predominately brick home sat empty until 1934, when Joseph Gilman moved in for one year. Finally in 1935, Clark and Margaret Wheeler purchased the home. They remained there into the 1990s. From the street, the home seems large enough, with its rather flat front made even taller in appearance by a steeply pitched roof. Here it is shown with the original rose climbers so popular at the time. (Courtesy of the Pickett-Wheeler family.)

A visiting relative of the Wheelers, Rose Anna Murphy Pickett, takes in the vast lawn while enjoying some sun. This photograph, taken from the side of the house, shows the extensive back wing of the home. Wheeler was an automobile insurance executive, one of the many industries that sprouted ancillary to the motorcar craze responsible for so many fortunes in the city. (Courtesy of Margaret Pickett.)

One room of the home originally built as an early version of a home theater was used as the Wheelers' trophy room. Note the large painting at center; it could be raised to reveal a screen for projector equipment on the room's opposite end. Big game hunting was a common pursuit among the wealthy in these years. Trips to far-flung lands almost always included time for hunting. When the house was sold, it is believed that the contents of the trophy room were donated to a local museum. (Courtesy of the Pickett-Wheeler family, image restoration by From Camera to Wall.)

The house at 4515 is an interesting take on the old style of architecture on North Meridian Street, featuring artfully placed large windows in an assortment of styles. Rendered with a contemporary twist, the home's overall appearance reflects its build date of 1957. The firm of Kopf & Wooling did a good job bridging time with this one. Owner Fred W. Morely was a businessman who served several terms on the merit board for the Marion County Sheriff's Department.

Fred W. Jenkins was an Indianapolis contractor who built 4519 for himself in 1924. The whimsical house, with its half-timbering treatment over a brick first story and lovely porte cochere, creates a nice juxtaposition between family-friendly and Old World elegant.

The Frank E. Gates home, at 4525, with a center chimney visually dividing the entry, is a handsome brick house. Gates, engaged in sales as a real estate broker, kept the home in his family through the next 50 years, leaving it to his sister Charlotte upon his passing.

Sited on a sloping lot, the 1953 ranch home of Elsworth and Irma Stucky at 4528 was landscaped in the fashion so popular when it was built. Shrubbery and foundation plantings of perennials were kept close to the home, allowing the wide expanse of uninterrupted grass to show off the lot's large size.

The home at 4531 belonged to investment banker William A. Umphrey for more than a dozen years. Built in 1923, it boasts a broad covered porch running almost the entire width of the facade. Deep overhangs and several trees likely helped keep the large foursquare cool during summer's oppressive heat in the years before home air-conditioning was available.

Samuel and Eunice Patterson built their dream home at 4536. The ranch was low-slung and spacious with the popular floorplan of the day so touted for entertaining at home. All modern conveniences were installed. The Pattersons moved into their home in 1956 and never looked back, enjoying it over the next several decades.

Listed among America's top 14 home builders by the Marion County Residential Builders Association and often referred to as "the Dean of Builders," Fred Palmer built 4544 on a steep hilltop lot as his own home. Palmer added a fully finished children's play area in the attic, an unusual use of space at the time. A few years later, Harold Ames, president of the Duesenberg Motor Car Company, purchased the home and kept his "Doozy" well maintained in the garage behind the house.

The stucco cottage at 4555 was designed in 1924 in the popular English country style by Thornton & Rodecker. Although it changed hands many times over the years, it seems the Dr. Wesley C. Ward family stayed the longest, starting in 1956 and living there over the next 10 years.

In 1952, this modern interpretation of a Colonial was built on a high corner lot at 4580. It was home for many years to Dr. Maynard K. Hines and his wife, Delia. Dr. Hines served as the first chancellor of Indiana University–Purdue University at Indianapolis and was the first Hoosier elected president of the American Dental Association.

Three

FORTY-SIXTH STREET THROUGH THE 5100 BLOCK

Samuel Falender chose this lot at 4605 to be next door to his brother Julius in 1920. Using the same architect, Merritt Harrison, and ideas gleaned from lavish Italian villas he admired in photographs, Falender filled his family home with fine textiles and modern amenities. The exterior was equally opulent, with a tiled roof, ornamental ironwork, and multiple sets of french doors. Polish-born and community-minded, Samuel Falender was the founder of the Beth El Congregation and the Beth El Men's Club.

Julius Falender was president and founder of Falender Iron and Scrap Metal. He and his brother Samuel also held a real estate investment concern. Julius commissioned Merritt Harrison to design this substantial Colonial at 4611 in 1919.

One of many ranch homes suddenly appearing on Meridian Street, 4617 popped up in 1952. A long list of occupants began with Earl W. Gibson, whose Meridian Street dream it seems was not long-lived, as the home was vacant by 1957. The term for these homes on the National Register application is "noncontributing structures." This is rather unfortunate, as all but one of the homes built during this period remain. They followed the same setbacks and lot size minimums demanded of earlier homes. High-quality materials and skilled professional builders and designers were employed, and most of the modern homeowners were sensitive to the landscaping and upkeep expectations of neighbors living in the long-established homes. As 4617 and its fellow members of the "Ranch Invasion" have passed the 50-year mark, they have settled in as a part of the history of the district and become more than noncontributing structures.

The John Madden home, at 4621, was known for its elegant furnishings for good reason. The John J. Madden Furniture Company manufactured upholstered goods in Indianapolis for more than 100 years, beginning in the 1880s. John's wife, Josephine, remained in this stylish abode into the 1950s.

The grand pillars of 4747 state its design style clearly as Colonial Revival, fitting for the president of an oil company. It was the home of the Russell S. Williams family for about 20 years.

Since 1975, Indiana's governors have called 4750 home—well, most have. During the Mitch Daniels administration, the family kept their personal home and used the official residence only for administrative offices. The house was renovated with updated wiring and central air-conditioning. Built in 1928, this is not the original house. The previous c. 1900 home was heavily damaged by a fire, and part of its foundation was used to build the house seen today. The first floor is open for organized tours, while the second floor is reserved as the private living quarters of the first family.

A long-time favorite along Meridian is Samuel O. Dungan's elaborate Tudor at 4801, quietly called "Dungan's Dungeon" by neighbors for the dark, brooding interior colors. The decor may have been intentionally subdued to contrast work and home for the successful owner of Polk's Sanitary Milk Company. Kinder visitors referred to the Dungan home as "the Milk House." Like other Meridian Tudors, 4801's exterior is merely a wrapper for the much-preferred modern floor plans of the day. These homes were built to impress from the curb, comfortably entertain large groups, and feel like home to family.

Rendered like a fancy French farmhouse, 4802 is rather straightforward in its treatment of brickwork, fenestration, and streamlined facade. The home was constructed in 1941 as attentions turned to the unsteady conditions around the globe, and once again a major war was on the horizon. The resulting design fits well with its neighbors but also lends an air of newness with its crisp lines.

When Schoen-Morgan built 4810 on speculation (a very common practice up and down the street) in 1937, it took a full two years to sell. But once the Leo E. Smith family bought the home, they stayed until the late 1970s. The pretty Colonial Revival held a timeless appeal for life insurance agent Leo, wife Arlvine, and their three children.

Certainly one of the most eye-catching features of 4814 is the intricately carved limestone balcony. The lacy openwork pattern contrasted by the substantial corner pieces is work rarely seen outside of Europe. It was home to the family of Indiana state representative Oscar A. Jose from 1934 to 1945. Jose was president of Midwestern Equity of Miami. A lot of Hoosier dollars at that time were being invested in South Florida.

One of the lots built upon more than once is 4821. The first home, a fashionable ranch, was built in 1950 for Edwin L. Cassady, president of Indianapolis Power and Light. The home was filled, not surprisingly, with every modern electric convenience available. It was sold in the 1990s, after the widowed Bernice Cassady moved on. The new owners undertook an extensive remodel of the property. Widely covered by local papers and television news, the failed update was eventually abandoned. The partially constructed, partially demolished house was deemed uninhabitable and torn down. Currently, 4821 is the site of a modern build, thoughtfully designed to take its place alongside the other beauties of Meridian Street.

When Woods Caperton, sales manager for the Eli Lilly Company, decided to build his dream home on Meridian Street in 1920, he wouldn't allow the placement of a five-year-old home owned by the Dow family to detour his plan. Caperton bought the property at 4830 and moved the Dow home around the corner to a lot on Forty-Ninth Street (effectively putting the home in its own backyard) to make room for his much grander redbrick Colonial.

The Brant-Weinhardt house, with its crenellated tower, anchors the northeast corner of Forty-Eighth and Meridian Streets. Variations in color in both the brick and the slate roof add texture and interest to some very large and otherwise plain expanses on the face of the home. However, with this artful use of visual texture and the bold tower, 4833 meets the standards of anyone's vision of the perfect Provençal home. Note that the heavy wooden entry door, located in the perfectly rounded tower, is curved to match.

The interior of 4833 was beautifully laid out to entertain and host events. In 1954, bride Helen Marie Weinhardt is surrounded by attendants as she prepares for her in-home wedding ceremony. (Courtesy of Alice Berger.)

Being home to the Democratic Party national chairman Frank McKinney, neighbors were not surprised to spot figures such as Pres. Harry Truman strolling along the sidewalk for a morning constitutional while visiting 4906. In addition to politics, McKinney had a hand in many businesses. He was chairman of American Fletcher Bank as well as co-owner of the Pittsburgh Pirates in partnership with celebrity crooner Bing Crosby.

J.J. Cole Jr. built 4909 on land he owned as a farm and weekend country retreat from the city. Going away to a northern lake community for the summer was not feasible, as he oversaw daily operations at the bustling Cole Motor Car Company. At the factory's peak, there were two large buildings (a three-story building and the initial five-story plant), and sales of the luxury autos were second only to Cadillac. (Courtesy of Frank N. and Patricia L. Owings.)

Historic home enthusiasts Frank and Patte Owings purchased a 1925 Cole Brunette shortly after buying 4909. In 1997, they successfully listed both the home and their car in the National Register of Historic Places. During their tenure as owners of the Cole home, the Owings graciously offered tours of their house and up-close looks at the Brunette for various charitable and neighborhood events. (Courtesy of Frank N. and Patricia L. Owings.)

The portico over 4919's entry floats high above the door on beautifully carved columns giving the illusion of a crown. The Burns & James–built home, known as the Baur-Booker house, was constructed in 1924. Baur was president of the Broad Ripple Park Company (an amusement park), Baur Tack, and Baur Realty, and director of Liquid Carbonic Gas. He also purchased the Terre Haute Brewery in 1933 to produce his Champagne Velvet beer.

Harry L. Freyn Sr., originally from Lawrenceburg, Indiana, owned the brick home designed by George & MacLucas at 4925 for 50 years (from 1924 to 1974). Freyn was a heating and plumbing contractor who founded his company in 1910 in Indianapolis. He also had a love for Thoroughbred horses. He owned and trained several and was very involved for years in Hollandale, Florida, serving as an officer of Gulfstream Race Track.

The stunning house at 4936, built in 1923, was home to internationally renowned thyroid specialist Dr. Goethe Link. As an old story goes, Dr. Link was chatting casually with Josiah "Joe" K. Lilly Jr. one day when Joe mentioned how he admired Link's new home on Meridian Street. At the time, Lilly and his wife, Ruth, lived three blocks to the west at 4050 Washington Boulevard in what was arguably a house equal in beauty. The Lillys were also actively building a new home, to be called Oldfields, on the grounds of the current Newfields (formerly the Indianapolis Museum of Art). By the end of the conversation, Lilly had convinced Link to trade homes by offering a substantial cash incentive. Joe and Ruth lived at 4936 for just over a year before they moved on to their new home with daughter Ruth and son Joe III. (Courtesy of Gertrude S. Rauch.)

No family held 4936 longer than the A.O. Reynolds family. This portrait with their beloved dogs gives an insider's view of life in one of the grandest homes on the street. The Reynolds family purchased the home in 1954 and owned it for over 50 years. From left to right are (first row) Anne, A.O. Sr., and A.O. Jr.; (second row) George, Jack, and Geoffrey. The dogs are Mark, Perky, Sean, and Misty. (Courtesy of the Rauch and Reynolds families.)

Behind 4936 stood this stunning children's playhouse, a miniaturized version of the homes streetside. In later years, the playhouse was torn down to make way for a more practical use of the space. (Courtesy of the Reynolds family.)

The Tudor styling of the Aufderheide-Culp house, at 4950, has become rather symbolic of the "Meridian Look." Rudolph Aufderheide was president of Commonwealth Loan Company. He sold his home to Stokely-VanCamp executive Charles C. Culp, whose family lived in the picturesque home until 1973. This house was featured on the cover of the 1992 book *The Main Stem: The History & Architecture of North Meridian Street*, published by Historic Landmarks Foundation of Indiana. The wildly popular book was written collaboratively by David J. Bodenhamer, Lamont Hulse, and Elizabeth B. Monroe. Now out of print, it featured a mix of vintage images borrowed from private and public collections, and the photographic talent of Marsh Davis.

The lovely porticoed home at 5001 is known as the Fairbanks-Buchanan. It was always a hub of activity. Early resident Richard M. Fairbanks had a busy and high-profile career in newspapers and broadcasting. Fairbanks moved his family four blocks north in 1926; six years later, the Paul H. Buchanan family purchased the home in 1932.

As seen here, the Buchanans really did treat this as a family home. Gatherings like this 1949 Easter celebration were often hosted at the spacious home. The family was quite social as well, knowing nearly everyone in town. The Buchanan family was a community staple, having established itself as the premier and trusted name in funeral homes serving Indianapolis for nearly 150 years. The business continues today, still in family hands. A mix of friends and family pauses for a group picture. (Courtesy of the Buchannon family.)

Built for entertaining in 1923 by H.L. Burns, the home's entry hall made a stunning impression on visitors. Many homes on Meridian feature the walk-under single or double staircase seen here.

Originally a guesthouse on the property of 5001, for many years the small house addressed as 5003 was known as the Honeymoon Cottage. The charming "micro-manse" often served as a first home to newlywed members of the Buchanan family. Inset at lower right are Charlene and Don Keller, residents of the cottage. (Courtesy of the Buchannon family.)

Château de Balleroy (purchased by Malcolm Forbes in 1970) in Normandy is thought to be the inspiration for 5008. Known as the Sears-Townsend house, this is one of the many stylistically interpretive homes Henry L. Simons built in the Meridian-Kessler neighborhood. Earl Sears, president of the Sears Cabinet Manufacturing Company, purchased this spec home from Simons in 1930. Later, the home was sold to author and Marion County prosecutor Earl Townsend, whose annual holiday display on the lawn featured a life-size Santa's sleigh complete with reindeer, a delight to Indianapolis children of all ages.

Known as the Evans-Blankenbaker house, 5019 was erected in 1901 as a summer cottage. Its existence as a respite from the heat and industry-fouled summer air of central Indianapolis was short-lived. In 1907, an extensive remodel added a second story and increased the overall living space substantially to make it a year-round family home presented as the stately Georgian Revival seen today. Although it was home to multi-term state senator Virginia Blankenbaker, the house gained some fame before the Blankenbakers moved in. The St. Margaret's Guild of City Hospital, then Wishard, and now Eskenazi, selected 5019 as its first decorator's show house in 1962. Currently in its 58th year, the St. Margaret's is the country's longest running event of its kind, even surpassing the famed Kipp's Bay by about 10 years. The home was turned over to local decorators and designers for several weeks to work their magic using the latest and most fashionable trends in home furnishings. Once the tickets were sold and the doors thrown open, the show house was an immediate success. Show houses have continued as an important fundraiser for the hospital.

The original farmhouse at 5050 served as a private school with an enhanced curriculum (considered groundbreaking and experimental at the time) from 1923 until 1926. The exclusive institution took the name Orchard School for its location on what was previously a large fruit tree grove cultivated by the Carey family. The school is still in existence just a few blocks away, where it has lost no luster as a prestigious place of learning. Mary Stewart Carey sold the farmland mere days before 1929's infamous Black Tuesday market crash. H.L. Simons scooped up this lot and others in spite of the economic downturn and built the home addressed as 5050 today.

Interiors up and down Meridian Street feature the famous Rookwood Tileworks ceramics in kitchens, hearths, sunrooms, and baths. Here, a snail-embellished soap dish is still in proud and stylish service since its installation in 1929. (Courtesy of Peggy Sabens.)

Like a fairytale castle, 5060 stands along Meridian Street as one of its medieval-modeled houses with a tower feature. Generally referred to as the Kobin-Nafe house, it was built in 1933. Henry V. Kobin, vice president of Real Silk Hosiery, lived in the home until it was purchased by Dr. Cleon A. Nafe and his wife, Eunice. Dr. Nafe was chief of surgery at Methodist Hospital and served on several boards including Blue Cross and Blue Shield, the Indianapolis Chamber of Commerce, and the Indianapolis Foundation, among others.

Beautiful formality and the crisp contrast of fresh white accented with a grass-green clay-tiled roof give 5104 a connection to the manicured lawn. It was built by Henry L. Simons in 1928 for Isaac E. Woodard, chairman of the Acme-Evans Flour Mill. A well-known and active member of the Quaker faith, Woodard, who graduated from Earlham College in 1904, later chaired the Earlham board of trustees.

The graceful 5105, built in 1930, was home to the John W. Esterline Sr. family for nearly three dozen years. Esterline made his mark in the business of electrical parts manufacturing as president of Esterline-Angus.

H.L. Simons–built 5110 was home to Indiana state senator Arthur R. Baxter from 1928 to 1964. Baxter was president of the Keyless Lock Company. The only firm of its kind, Keyless, based in Indianapolis, had more than 50 fulltime salesmen on the road selling complete post office interior installations across the country. The manufacturing plant, also located in Indianapolis, could produce a complete post office (everything from lockable "keyless" boxes rentable to patrons to teller stations to stately desks for postmasters) in one day.

Another H.L. Simons home, 5111 sits directly across the street from 5110. It was built in 1929. Real estate investment executive Berkley Duck and his wife, Louise, lived here for about 10 years before Berkley suffered a sudden cardiac event and died. The widow moved her children to a smaller home she had built down the street at 4455. Later, Frederic M. Ayres Jr. of the L.S. Ayres Department Stores lived here.

Dr. John F. Rigg built this stately
brick and limestone home with a
dignified air at 5115 in 1936 and
stayed for 20 years, raising his
children before selling and moving
to Florida to eventually retire. Dr.
Rigg, a graduate of Indiana University
Medical School, was a general
surgeon and a charter member of the
National Society of Family Practice.

One of the Meridian Street homes
built with its front entry facing
away from the busy street, 5125 is
particularly pretty from the curb
with a large sunroom anchoring the
street end. A porch railing sits atop
this room, inviting ideas of cool
summer evenings spent gazing past
the tree canopy at the stars. The
home was built in 1925 for Benjamin
F. Hoe, a real estate investor.

Covered in a tawny-toned brick and perched atop a slight hill among several trees, this 1930 house at 5130 was the home of Louis P. Wolf, president of H.P. Wasson Department Stores after the retirement of his father, Arthur, in 1963. It is one of the street's most handsome homes from the curb, and one can assume it was equally well outfitted inside. Wasson's was a premier department store alongside L.S. Ayres and the William H. Block Company. Serving central Indiana from 1874 to 1980 under three separate owners, Wasson's was the first of the "Big Three" to be consumed by larger chains and eventually disappear.

Local television news anchor and media personality Mike Ahern lived at 5140 for nearly 30 years. Another of H.L. Simons's continental interpretations, this one uniquely has a third-story glassed artist's studio. Sitting above the mature tree canopy surrounding the house, this room was flooded with light and perfect for an artist's discerning tastes in color-mixing perfection.

Combinations of painted and stained fine woods as ornamentation abound up and down the historic street. Here, inside 4136, is a rare combination of barrel vaulted and bent beamed natural wood ceiling crowns with board and batten paneled walls painted in their original white. (Courtesy of the Schaller family.)

Despite its full-on charm and curb appeal, 5141 sat empty for over a year after it was completed in 1930. Likely, buyers were a bit reticent and skittish. It was purchased in 1932 by Bert McBride, although the stockbroker moved around the corner to a home on East Fifty-Second Street within a few years.

Built by Simons as the great crash of 1929 was still stinging, 5145 was home to Dr. John and Bertha Carmack. The Carmacks had a stately home on Fall Creek Road just to the south, but as Dr. Carmack had just received a promotion at Methodist Hospital, he surprised his wife with the larger home, better suited for modern entertaining, on moving day. Imagine her surprise when she woke to movers packing her belongings without notice and then ended the day sleeping in a grand new house.

From 1924 until 1980, this home at 5148 was only owned by two families. The Grossarts held it through two generations until 1940. Charles A. Grossart was the Marion County auditor. Attorney Clair McTurnan then purchased the house, and his family remained there for the next 40 years.

H.L. (Henry) Simons, the most prolific builder of homes along Meridian Street, was very much a self-made man. He designed and built 5151 as his own home with upscale appeal and durable materials usually reserved for commercial and public buildings in 1923. He so believed in the vision of the streetscape he and many others were creating that he continued to buy up lots and build homes on a speculative basis throughout the Great Depression.

Here, the much-overworked H.L. Simons (second from left, wearing a hat) takes time out for his favorite leisure activity. This photograph of Simons was snapped while golfing with visiting big-league slugger Babe Ruth (far left) at Woodstock Country Club, where many Meridian families held membership. The remaining three men are unidentified. (Courtesy of Peggy Sabens.)

Four

FIFTY-SECOND STREET NORTH TO FIFTY-FIFTH STREET

Russian immigrant Rudolph Domont capitalized on the burgeoning thirst of industrial workers in Indianapolis and neighboring areas by producing Pepsi-Cola. Though the Domont family home at 5201 seems rather modest compared to some of the neighboring properties, the size and economy fell right into line with Domont's knack for frugality and sharp money acumen. The family enjoyed living in their charming half-timbered cottage for about 10 years.

Not unlike several other homes along Meridian Street, the house formerly addressed as 5204 faces a cross street, where its driveway access falls as well. For some reason, 5204 was renumbered as 2 West Fifty-Second Street, while all the others with the same situation of lot placement retain their addresses on Meridian Street.

The house at 5207 was first lived in by Harrly L. Dipple, who built the home in 1920. The second owners, Rev. Howard Cadle and his wife, Ola, only had a brief stay of about five years. Reverend Cadle came swiftly to prominence as he used the country's new medium, broadcast radio, to spread his gospel messages far and wide.

Often credited as the father of televangelists, Cadle was wildly popular locally and nationwide. He built his enormous Cadle Temple (the largest church of its time) with seating for 10,000 at the corner of New Jersey and Ohio Streets. (Courtesy of the Boetcher family.)

The house at 5211, an appealing addition to the block in 1952, was the home of Ross Ottinger. Though comparatively modern in styling, elements of American Colonial and the steep roof pitch blend the home nicely with surrounding ones. Ottinger was a surgeon, originally from nearby Whitestown, who specialized in abdominal procedures. He served at Methodist Hospital for more than 50 years.

In 1920, a frame house was built at 5217 for the Samuel T. Brown family. Brown was president of Brown Brothers Inc. The firm published sheet music, mostly religious, and mostly written by one family member or another, and also brokered teas and coffees.

Curbside formality was often repeated in the layout and landscaping of back lawns. This pleasing yet simple design's symmetry is both formal and versatile. (Courtesy of the Bucchanon family.)

Physician Frank W. Cregor bought 5220, an H.L. Simons–built home, in 1934, two years after it was finished. In addition to being a prominent Indianapolis dermatologist, Cregor served in the state senate for one term. He also taught dermatology at Indiana University Medical School and was head of the state health department while serving 10 years on the judicial committee of the American Medical Association.

For formal entertainment, luxurious furnishings and carefully selected antiques were the decor de rigueur. Here, a pair of hand embroidered chairs covered in fine silk flank the fireplace at 5354. (Courtesy of Peggy Sabens.)

James M. Drake, president of the Empire Life and Casualty Company, bought this H.L. Simons home soon after it was finished in 1932. Later, Theodore Marbaugh, the president of Columbia Construction and the related company M&D Builders, and his wife, Mary, purchased 5230 and called it home.

Vern C. Vanderbilt swooped up 5235, a ranging Tudor built by Simons. A fascinating and innovative man, Vanderbilt built his own automobile while in grade school using a junk washing machine motor and is often credited as the inventor of cruise control. He helped design the P-51 Mustang, World War II's fastest piston-engine fighter, and was even instrumental in compressing the tablets of Alka Seltzer with a consistent and reliable manufacturing method.

William and Mildred Sandmann put up this rather French-inspired one-story home in 1949. While living at 5240, William Sandmann was chairman of the Marshall-Huschart Machinery Company. He also served as director of First Federal Savings and Loan.

Felix M. McWhirter, a prominent Indianapolis banker, lived at 5241 for several years. McWhirter was president of Marion County's first state-chartered bank, People's Bank, at the age of 28. The bank was founded by his father, Felix T. McWhirter, in 1891, and Felix M. was handed the reins upon his father's death. He successfully guided the bank until he retired to the Phoenix area, where he died at 97 still holding the title of chairman emeritus of People's Bank & Trust Company.

E.J. Baker was the first owner of 5243, staying only long enough for his home at 5265 to be completed about a year later. His family was engaged in several industries in the Indianapolis area.

Evocative of an Old South plantation house with its dual walk-up to the first-floor entry, 5250 was built for Clemen and Zuleme Mueller. Later, it was home to local political figure Linda Sue Gilman.

Clarence A. Cook purchased 5252, another of H.L. Simons's homes built on speculation in 1930 with irresistible storybook appeal. Cook, a graduate of DePauw University, was an insurance broker for many years and a vice president and board member of the Bankers Trust Company. During the Theodore Roosevelt administration, Cook was called upon by the president to help organize the insurance department of Washington's Bureau of Corporations. The family made their home here over the next 30 years.

The house at 5260 takes full advantage of mixed materials, multiple surface treatments on the facade, and a staggered streetside footprint. The result is one of the most admired H.L. Simons homes in the district. It was finished in 1930 and is often referred to as the MacGill-Wemmer house. Its first occupant, Robert A. MacGill, was manager of all branch offices in Indiana for the Crane Company, manufacturer of plumbing and heating building supplies. William Wemmer, the second owner, was an attorney and a one-time candidate for mayor of Indianapolis.

E.J. Baker moved into 5265, an expansive home built for his family, after a scant two years at their previous address next door at 5243. It must have been quite the adventure to watch their future home rise out of the ground on the adjoining lot.

Publishing executive and noted Hoosier historian D. Laurance Chambers of the Bobbs-Merrill Company moved his family into the showy Simons-built Tudor at 5272 during the late 1920s. His publishing house produced the works of internationally beloved James Whitcomb Riley (a frequent guest of Chambers) and Raggedy Ann creator Johnny Gruelle, who lived a few blocks east on College Avenue. Ayn Rand is said to have been a frequent guest of the Chambers family as well.

Walter E. Wolf, president of H.P. Wasson department stores, and his wife, Tekla, built 5275 in 1928. Wolf later moved to a position of chairman of Wasson's when his son took over day-to-day operations as president. During World War II, Tekla took up the task of directing the city's Victory Garden program.

The house at 5300 was built in 1930 for James S. Watson. Watson was vice president of the Link Belt company, which manufactured chain mechanisms for industry. His traditional Meridian Street home of brick and limestone was framed by several old-growth trees in the front yard when built.

The pretty house at 5320 was home to a man who literally changed the world. Harley W. Rhodehamel, a chemist working at the Eli Lilly Company, discovered a method for manufacturing insulin, thus effectively changing the lives of diabetics worldwide. Rhodehamel was himself a diabetic.

The Yuncker home, at 5323, has more than doubled in size since it was built in 1924. The current owners added an artfully done and nearly seamless addition to the home beginning in the late 1990s. Built for the James Yuncker family, it was a center of entertainment for a variety of guests.

Yuncker owned what was once the world's largest Coca-Cola bottling plant. The elaborate art deco building was eventually abandoned, and operations were moved to a modern facility adjacent to the Indianapolis Motor Speedway. For the next several years, the large campus was used as a maintenance hub servicing and storing school buses for Indianapolis Public Schools. Currently, the property and buildings are being repurposed as a luxury hotel, upscale eateries, and boutique shopping. Known for its decadent and sanitary interior, pictured here is a bit of the decorative stone production floor in Coke signature red and white.

The limestone walls with bronze gates and lights were added in 1932, about eight years after the Yunckers moved into their new home. Years later, Bruce and Denise Cordingley donated their streetside wall and gates as a preservation easement to Historic Landmarks Foundation. This act of generosity and foresight assures protection and preservation of this section of exceptional streetscape.

Another H.L. Simons home, this one at 5330 appears to have been planted onto its lot long before 1931. Substantial in size, formality, and aesthetic appeal, the home is one of Meridian Street's most admired addresses. Two years after the speculation home was finished, it was purchased by William and Anna Zumpfe. He was a career loan and investment banker who also enjoyed directing orchestras.

Though builder H.L. Simons threw all of his beloved embellishments into the design of 5335 when he built it in 1928, the house stood vacant for two long years after it was finished. Finally, Dr. Bernays Kennedy purchased the home. Dr. Kennedy had served as a major in the medical corps during World War I. In the summer of 1935, he traveled north to Minnesota to escape the city heat. He had been ill for several years and was frail. He died while in Duluth visiting a cousin.

Known as the Hugh Love House, 5354 is perhaps the best-preserved home in the district. The house has changed hands only three times since it was built in 1929. Remarkably, each resident has perhaps added a bit to the interior decor of the home but never taken away any of the original flourishes. All wallpapers, tile, cabinetry, flooring, and fixtures are original to the home. Draperies have only been replaced with identical designs. But rather than feeling like a museum, the home somehow remains tastefully current, proof that good design is indeed timeless.

Designed by architect F. Foltz for Richard E. Foltz, 5360 is a large four-columned Colonial interpretation built to blend in with neighboring homes when added in 1953. Engineer John Bennett Wilson and wife Eunice purchased the home in 1955 and owned it for more than 40 years.

Having grown up at 5525, Sallie Reahard built this tasteful American cottage at 5363 for herself and her elderly father around 1953. The much larger family home had become too cumbersome for the ailing Ralph. The high corner lot and tall dense hedge provided both a sound barrier and a soothing refuge to the nature-loving Reahard. Known widely for her interest in conservation and generous philanthropy, she lived a busy but simple existence. Her expenditures were never extravagant. Many were shocked at the enormous endowments she left to charities in her will, and the newspapers at the time were fast to call her a recluse. However, those who knew her saw her differently and spoke of her unassuming demeanor and work ethic for causes she passionately supported, such as nature preserves and children's health.

The house at 5401 made its debut on the street in 1952 as a story-and-a-half home originally built for Paul L. McCord. Extensive renovations have since taken place, and a full second story has been added, including volume over the original single-story entry.

In 1938, architect Herbert Foltz designed this handsome Colonial for Walter R. Foltz, who owned Midland Building Industries. With its impressive two-story columns and rich red brick, 5402 is a lovely example of the Colonials so popular in the 1930s.

Pulitzer Prize–winning author Meredith Nicholson (*The House of 1,000 Candles*, 1905) lived at 5417 until he was called to the service of his country. In 1932, he was appointed US ambassador to Peru under the Roosevelt administration. Immediately following his Peru assignment, Nicholson went on to serve as minister to Paraguay, Venezuela, and Nicaragua. Later, the Warren Fairbanks family (son of Theodore Roosevelt's vice president, Charles Fairbanks) purchased 5417. Fairbanks made his fortune as president of the *Indianapolis News*, Fairbanks Broadcasting Company, and many other business interests.

The home at 5420 was constructed in 1924 to intentionally seem decades older, as was popular with buyers. The scene-stealer for this home is the amazing leaded and crested window dwarfing the entry door. Multiple chimneys add additional opportunity for dimension and interest as they peek out from behind the large shrubbery buffer between the home and passing traffic.

The Morris L. Brown family enjoyed more than 20 years at this hilltop home designed by Burns & James in 1936. Later, William and Frances Kennedy, who lived up the street at 5655, purchased the home. The original porte cochere of 5425 was removed in the 1970s.

In 1929, Dr. Perry E. Powell and his wife, Louise, began building speculative homes on Meridian Street. Louise Powell had an excellent eye for popular design, and Dr. Powell fully supported her efforts. They successfully completed and sold 5420, 5430, and 5440 before the market crash of that same year. Plans they had to build five more homes were scrapped, and they did not return to building. They lived here in 5430 for several years.

Nationally syndicated cartoonist Kin (Frank McKinney) Hubbard moved his family from the fashionable Indianapolis neighborhood of Irvington to 5437 in 1928. He was widely adored for his political satire and uniquely Hoosier wit and wisdom dished up by character Abe Martin.

The house at 5440, with its imposing dual chimney, is a study in formality and Old World grace. It was built by Dr. and Mrs. P.E. Powell in 1929 on speculation, and the couple lived in the home for a few years before they were able to sell it. Eventually, it was purchased by Minna H. Block, widow of Meir Block. Meir's father, William H. Block, founded the upscale department store chain of the same name. Meir managed the multistore chain with his two brothers until his passing. Considered one of the "Big Three" department stores in Indianapolis, Block's was the second to be consumed via buyout by a larger chain, leaving only L.S. Ayres to survive for a few years.

The Schoen-Morgan Company built 5455 in 1930, but it was only occupied as a rental until three years later. Harry and Nellie Noel purchased the ornate house with its formulaic Tudor style consisting of brick, half-timbering, and limestone.

Five

5500 TO THE INDIANAPOLIS CENTRAL CANAL

At 5500, the campus of Meridian Street United Methodist Church consumes several acres. Built in 1950, the design and siting were carefully planned by Russ & Harrison to observe setbacks and blend architecturally with the surrounding homes. One of only three structures in the historic district not serving as a single-family residence, most would agree that it has been a welcome neighbor.

The last single-family dwelling to be built in the historic district until the 1990s was this Colonial Revival at 5501, designed by Jack Albershardt in 1966 and sold to A. Lee Clifford in 1968. The Cliffords divided their time between Indianapolis and Naples, Florida, from 1947 onwards.

Edward Pierre mixed together several elements to produce 5519 with its storybook charm in 1928. No doubt due to unfortunate timing, it remained empty until 1930, when it was sold to Hall and Ruth Keeling. The Keelings kept the home nearly 40 years.

Built in 1930 on speculation, 5520 was eventually in use from 1956 until the late 1980s as the Methodist church's Sunday school. Around 1990, the house was sold and renovated, returning it to its intended use as a single-family home.

The Ralph M. Reahard home, at 5525, was built in 1929. Reahard, who started at Eli Lilly as a chemist and rose to the position of vice president, lived in the home for more than 20 years with his family. By 1953, Ralph, a widower, was in failing health, and the large home was of cumbersome arrangement. He and his daughter Sallie built a one-story home at 5363, sold the too-big family home at 5525, and moved on.

Max Katz built 5530 in a nicely balanced ranch format in 1949. Moving from nearby Delaware Street, Katz, the owner of Max Katz Bags, wanted a modern space for entertaining family and the ease one-story living offered. Katz was a founder and board member of the Jewish National Fund.

The Jacobean beauty at 5540 was built in 1930 by one of America's top residential contractors, Fred L. Palmer. Owned by the Potts family from 1931 to 1935, it was eventually the home of Carl and Erma Sauer. Carl Sauer, a well-known engineer, wrote the locally loved autobiography *Engineering a Life*. In honor of his memoir, Mayor Stephen Goldsmith proclaimed October 9, 1994, Carl Sauer Day. Sauer was also awarded the state's highest honor, Sagamore of the Wabash, on that same day by Gov. Evan Bayh.

Built in 1930, the lovely Old World–looking 5545 was home to Dr. David Lozow and his wife, Betty, in the 1950s and 1960s until the ranch home at 5677 became available. It was not uncommon for folks to live in more than one of these homes. Meridian Street was a lifestyle as much as an address, even prompting several old-timers to move into the once-protested modern ranches or Tarkington Towers when they decided to sell their longtime family homes.

The house at 5548 is a well-sited and -landscaped ranch built by Wendell and Barbara Taylor during the modern invasion of 1953. The couple worked in publishing for several years. Upon the death of Wendell's father, he assumed the role of president of Taylor Bookkeeping.

Built in 1937, the impressive home at 5555 was at the north end of the district and also at the end of the timeline for building truly large, showy, and meant-to-impress homes. David Layton, a general insurance agent with much success, lived here with his wife, Glenn, until 1943.

Tom and Viola Noble found their Meridian Street dream home in the form of a modern ranch at 5556, built in 1953. Viola kept the home after Tom's passing until 1960.

The house at 5557 is uniquely mixed in a fantasy of architectural styles. The result is a stunning appearance with lots of curb appeal. This was the trademark style of H.L. Simons. Built in 1936 for Clyde and Mary Dibble, the home remained in the Dibble family for about 30 years. He worked for the New York Central Railroad as vice president in charge of storage.

Ralph W. and Grace Showalter bought 5601 in 1934, three years after it was finished. Ralph, a 1909 graduate of Purdue University, went to work at Eli Lilly as a chemist. He retired as head of the foreign sales department. Grace headed the Marion County War Finance Commission during World War II, coordinating the sale of war bonds. Although Hollywood actress Carole Lombard spent her last night at the downtown Claypool Hotel rather than as a guest at the Showalter home, Mary was likely one of the last people to speak with the starlet before she died tragically when her plane crashed near Las Vegas while en route to Hollywood. Her promotion of the war bond effort during her Indianapolis sweep yielded sales of $12 million (an astounding equivalent of about $206 million today).

This stunning stone home was built in 1938. Glenn F. Warren occupied 5606 for the first 10 years after it was built. He owned Hotel Warren, more commonly known as the Canterbury. A downtown institution, the swanky hotel did business for several years as the Lockerbie before Warren purchased it. It featured the Viking Tap Room and 250 rooms with upscale amenities such as a private bath and radio in every room.

The contemporary home at 5616 was built in 1953 for Myron and Harriet Wolf. The Wolfs owned several fast food restaurant franchises around the central Indiana area. These included Captain D's and Wendy's locations.

F.M. Bartholomew designed 5617, a lovely Norman-influenced home, in 1936 for Robert and Eva Moore. Robert Moore was a prominent cardiologist and served as a professor at the Indiana University School of Medicine.

Warm and inviting 5627 was built for the Dimitri Meditch family in 1936. They held the home for nearly 40 years. Meditch was founder and chairman of the board of National Wholesale Grocery Company. Coming to the United States as a youngster from Macedonia, he put himself through college at prestigious Valparaiso University.

At a time when most new construction on Meridian Street was in the popular mid-century modern style, 5630 was built in 1953 by Abe Kroot to blend in with its "old guard" neighbors. With four gleaming fluted columns supporting a deep portico, the Kroot family's home is often mistaken for a 1930s vintage. Abe was president of Joseph Kroot Company, a scrap processing firm.

Frank K. Levinson had 5639 built in 1930. Levinson often said that he built the incredibly sophisticated home for a grand total of $20,000. He was president of the Harry Levinson stores. A long-time brand known for quality service and professional sales staff, the single-location retailer of hats that opened in downtown Indianapolis grew to be the most successful men's clothier in the market. With a peak of 114 stores all over the Midwest, Levinson's was every gentleman's go-to for fashion and quality. After 90 years of robust growth, the chain folded in 1995.

The elegance of 5650 is played against the inviting informality of the balustraded front patio. The home was built in 1929 for Arthur Valinetz, president of the Lincoln Jewelry and Loan Company. A few years later, Clarence and Marjory Alig moved into the spacious and impressive home. A veteran of World War I, Clarence was president of the Home Land Investment Company and vice president of his family's long-established Home Stove Company, originally located in Greenfield, Indiana.

The Dr. Sidney S. Aronson family lived at 5655 for several years. In the late 1960s, the home was gutted and extensively remodeled after it was damaged and in need of repair. Built in 1938 but gutted to the exterior walls, this is perhaps Meridian Street's "newest" old house.

After moving from 5655, the Aronsons came across the street to the newly built 5670 in 1949. A veteran of both world wars, Sidney Aronson spent his career focused on diseases and conditions of the ears, nose, throat, and eyes. He was credited with the invention of many medical tools and was a founding member of Broadmoor Country Club.

The heavily treed lot of 5675 may have been part of the attraction when the William B. Miller family chose it in 1949. Miller was a lawyer who practiced in partnership with his brother. As deputy prosecutor, he was part of the team that prosecuted and successfully convicted many in the 1920s Ku Klux Klan trials in Indianapolis.

One of the most modern houses on Meridian Street, almost cubist in appearance, 5677 was home to Melvin Lichtenberg when built in 1953. The next owners came from a few doors down in 1966, when Dr. David Lozow and his wife, Betty, moved from their Old World two-story into this futuristic home with a private swimming pool.

The design of the charming cottage at 5678 is credited to Nina C. Mann. Her father, F.O. Mann, was a well-established contractor at the time. It was built in 1925 for the Mann family's own use. Nina Mann continued working for her father for many years. She was particularly talented at selecting desirable lots to build homes on.

Sadie and Sanders Klein's mid-century modern ranch at 5681 is interesting because of its artful placement on the slightly rolling lot. Sanders Klein was a partner at the M.S. Cassen accounting firm. A native of New York City, he made his home here in Indianapolis for 23 years.

The J. Harry Miles home, at 5690, is another one where the original owner sold and then later repurchased the home. Built in that hard year of 1930, the home was vacant for three full years before the Miles family bought it in 1933. They only stayed for two years, and the home had two more owners over the next three years. It then sat unoccupied again for another five years. In 1947, Harry Miles once again bought the home, and remained there until 1974.

Nestled on a high bank on a sloping lot, this shingled home, built in 1922, evokes the old homes of colonial New England. It was home to John L. Mutz for several years. He was controller at Hoosier Food Systems, a holding company of more than two dozen Burger Chef restaurants in Indiana and Kentucky. He was also father of John M. Mutz, who served as Indiana lieutenant governor to Robert D. Orr. The house, at 5693, is known for its exceptional view and feeling of living in the treetops.

One of the three structures in the district not in use as a single-family residence, 5694 is also the oldest structure remaining. Built as a log-walled farmhouse around 1900, the home has steadily served as a restaurant since about 1920. Although the name and ownership have changed many times (Dodd's Townhouse and the Flagpole, among others), and fire has caused need for extensive repairs and remodels, the restaurant, as the Meridian, is still thriving as a neighborhood favorite. (Courtesy of Lux Restaurants.)

A section of an original log-sided wall was revealed when Lux Restaurants added aesthetic upgrades to the Meridian. Diners can touch a piece of history or perhaps, as some claim, have a fleeting encounter with Alice "Polly" Carter, the original lady of the house and friendly apparition.

Alice Carter Park, an odd triangle of land at the northwesternmost tip of the historic district, was once the property of Albert and Polly Carter, the couple who built 5694. When Albert sold the home, he donated the corner in his wife's name to be used as a park for residents to socialize and enjoy as a waypoint during daily strolls. Prolific upscale home builder O.C. Winters owned a small section of land at the south edge of the park for many years. In 1999, his widow, Jeanette Winters, donated the parcel, expanding the little park. One of the many benches installed there is inscribed with a quote selected by resident Peggy Sabens from Booth Tarkington's *Magnificent Ambersons*. Intended to honor the Winters family's generosity, the quote also sums up life along this street of beautiful homes succinctly: "Most of the trees had been left to flourish still, and, at some distance, or by moonlight, the place was in truth beautiful."

Designed by John Parish in the late 1950s, the Daniel and Marie Anderson home, at 5701, is southern facing at the corner of Meridian and Fifty-Seventh Streets. Constructed in a symmetrical arrangement in a deep-toned brick, the one-story home is tastefully adorned with contrasting shutters and a pleasing roofline.

Ronald Platt designed 5707 for Joseph and Norma Cripe. The home has a large amount of space with separate areas for family life and formal entertaining—just what all the homemaking magazines of 1952 were touting as desirable in homebuilding and ranch efficiency.

Ronald Platt designed and built a second home at 5715 simultaneous to 5707. Sited on the lot to be deeper than it is wide, this is an equally roomy ranch house. The single-story house was so popular after World War II because of economic and cultural changes. The days of carriage houses serving as detached garages with servants' quarters above or tucked under the eaves of a finished attic were fading. Refrigeration no longer required ice blocks, supermarkets replaced corner grocers and the bustling stalls at City Market, and laundry was done in-house using machines that also could fluff and dry. The life of ladies along Meridian Street was becoming more modern and much less carefree.

Built in 1909 in the middle of a 200-acre farm, the Dr. Onis Brendel house, at 5723, still looks very much at home on Meridian Street today. Dr. Brendel spent only a brief time practicing medicine in Indianapolis before he returned to his nearby hometown of Zionsville, where he enjoyed a 40-year career.

The last of the modern homes built in the northern tip of the district came along in 1955. John Parish sidestepped his previous, more modern designs with 5735 and gave the Darlington family a more traditional aesthetic. The spacious home blends well with its neighbors.

Nearing the canal, 5741 stands out with its tall face and three equal dormers perched atop a steep slate roof. City directories list James and Lillian Trindle as having lived here. Lillian's widowed sister Blanche E. Kipp lived with them in the brick and limestone beauty, built in 1934. James was employed by the Steam Railroad.

Upon entering the district from the north, be sure to look west for a glimpse of 5747. The Ingles home was built in 1932 and is locally referred to as the Juliet House for the large curved top front window with a balcony. The Ingles family was not the first to live in the home, but they stayed there for nearly 50 years. (Courtesy of Sarah Lebron.)

Overjoyed and celebrating with a playful dance, Jim and Mary Ingles are pictured after their purchase of 5747. They bought the home from original owner Theodore VanGestel. (Courtesy of Sarah Lebron.)

A young Jane Vernatler Daniel poses on the famed Juliet balcony for a photograph. The house was always a gathering place for family and hosted many holidays and weddings. It is a worthy home to welcome visitors entering the district from the north or to usher them out after ending a tour from the south. (Courtesy of the Ingles family.)

DISCOVER THOUSANDS OF LOCAL HISTORY BOOKS
FEATURING MILLIONS OF VINTAGE IMAGES

Arcadia Publishing, the leading local history publisher in the United States, is committed to making history accessible and meaningful through publishing books that celebrate and preserve the heritage of America's people and places.

Find more books like this at
www.arcadiapublishing.com

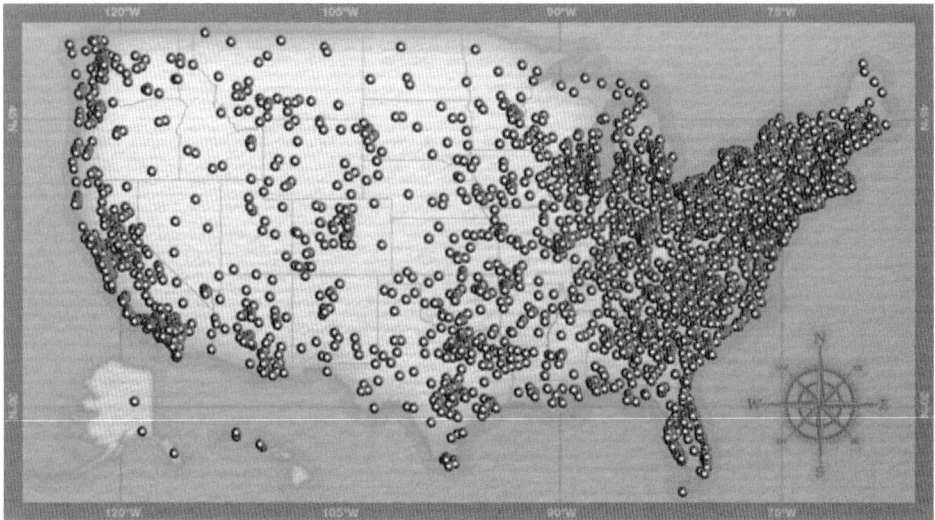

Search for your hometown history, your old stomping grounds, and even your favorite sports team.